WE CAN'T
EVER
DO THIS
AGAIN

WE CAN'T
EVER
DO THIS
AGAIN

AMBER McMILLAN

poems

A Buckrider Book

Buckrider Books is an imprint of Wolsak and Wynn Publishers.

Cover and interior design: Natalie Olsen, Kisscut Design
Author photograph: Nathaniel G. Moore
Typeset in Mercury Text by Hoefler & Co.
Printed by Coach House Printing Company Toronto, Canada

The publisher gratefully acknowledges the support of the Canada Council for the Arts, the Ontario Arts Council and the Canada Book Fund.

Buckrider Books
280 James Street North
Hamilton, ON
Canada L8R 2L3

Library and Archives Canada Cataloguing in Publication

McMillan, Amber, 1981–, author
We can't ever do this again / Amber McMillan.

Poems.
ISBN 978-1-894987-99-8 (pbk.)

I. Title.

PS8625.M52W43 2015   C811'.6   C2015-900832-8

For Paul Van Veen

(1926–2011)

We stand at the prow again of a small ship

anchored late at night in the tiny port

looking over to the sleeping island: the waterfront

is three shuttered cafés and one naked light burning.

To hear the faint sound of oars in the silence as a rowboat

comes slowly out and then goes back is truly worth

all the years of sorrow that are to come.

JACK GILBERT
"A Brief For The Defense"

PART
—1—

PART
—2—

PART
—3—

PART
—4—

PART
—1—

PEACE

I can hear the blown-out tire on the 401,
the coon fight where the smaller one
lost an eye — the good one — the renovations
on the neighbour's upstairs rental unit,
cicadas, still the goddamn cicadas, unbelievably,
into November, all those Catholic school kids —
twelve and thirteen years old — colliding
into one another, into the street, into the air,
your voice, "I meant what I said," three times
in three minutes, I heard you, but you mistook
the silence for peace (either mine or your own),
my shoulder too, throbbing for weeks, maybe
months, that neighbour and those guitars, he
hangs them on the only wall completely visible
from the street, as if he isn't inviting jealousy,
alarmed when he is robbed blind two and a half
weeks later. It's true there's a war, and those kids,
at least some of those kids, have grief, more
than they should, have an indefensible father,
or a deal in the works, the consistent buzz of your
still-running engine, air through the ventilation
system, there are my big plans too, and all
the money I have or don't have, that my grandfather
is dead, died in the spring, eaten by a cancer
of the body — not the other kind — for a year
he was dying, and then finally he did, left his wife,
his kids, left his house, left me — the trick
is the shift, *progress*, otherwise the whole thing,
this and everything else, is a disaster.

TABLE TALK

On the sly, you had described me to your pal
as an unwed young mother, somewhat admirable,
if a bit sad. You relayed the details of my life
as you know them, halfway fact and halfway plan.
The secret might have kept, but the minute you
left for the can, your friend finked in my ear:
I expected you to be a teenager, his breath hot
on my face, and the small wet debris from
the inside of his mouth dampened my cheek.
My turned cheek. My half-cheek. My halfway
in and halfway out cheek, cocked at an intimate
angle meant to encourage him to keep talking,
but to talk to me slowly, to drop his voice
to the lowest, most private register possible.

BRYSON, QUEBEC, 1996

The question of which is worse
is complicated more by the following
things: I know what I saw. Bright
headlights swept the forest corner
where the thick wood met the road.

I saw the man or ghost boy or boyish
girl caught in the sweep, front-lit
for no more than a second, squatting
on a flat belly between pine trees
and brush, the dark pitch of foliage

shadowed and skewed by the beam.
I saw his or her shirt, button-down,
his or her pants, black, and glassy
glasses, then at the ambit, the car
slide around the corner leaving it all

still again, everything exactly as it
had been before the headlights.
A child myself, the choice became
to remain paralyzed on the road
in terror, or to give in to the sharp

quake of adrenalin meant to mobilize
survival, to run as fast as possible up
the steep hill to your house where
you are sure to greet me sidelong,
drunk-shot and gearing for a fight.

It's a non-choice but I made it,
running for what I thought was my life,
and then to you: manic, scribbling
at the dining room table — a letter,
you told me later, to an infuriated

teacher who had a hand in your
recent termination from the school:
There's no such thing as ghosts, dear.
What there are, are crazy people sitting
in the woods in the middle of the night.

SONNET XXI

The day you visited a doctor in Victoria, diagnosed
with arthritis and liver deterioration, you told me
you stopped in Duncan to stand up after driving
for hours. You'd pulled into the gas station in Nanoose
having spotted a recent copy of *GQ*. You said it was
the *GQ* that made you think of me, there, where
the people live miles apart in small wooden homes
haphazardly stationed among liquor stores, food marts
and abandoned churches. An afterthought of a town,
or a mistake they're trying to make the best of.
That is also where Opa died in his wooden home,
a place not unlike the church where those thin
cardboard stars hung on the wall during Neela's violin
recital; one of the things that brought you to tears.

VICTORY LAP

for Spencer

I wanted to give you this friendship
bracelet, a lanyard wire or a flossed
half hitch knot, a Broken Ladder,
an Inverse Chevron or Totem Pole.
It could have been the Flip Flop Zig Zag
or Candy Stripe too, right before
the razzle-dazzle of the strobe lights
when the speaker took the stage to say
It cannot be that death is the worst;
it's more around the edges that hurts
then pinned what remained of his speech
to the belly of the podium — a gesture
that looked like generosity, though it wasn't.

A WAGER

In 1949, the middle-aged and sufficiently
well-mannered educators and nurses
at the Fernald School in Massachusetts
famously provided their developmentally
challenged students with radioactive oatmeal —
the city-funded leg of a state-funded project —
to determine the precise amount of swill
the human body could take before collapse.

Three times daily the children gathered
in the bustling school cafeteria, regularly
chasing one another, pushing, poking, tripping,
then finally settling on the long wooden
benches lining the lunch tables outfitted
with stacks of ceramic bowls and Lucite
water glasses, neatly embossed with postwar
airplanes and topped with desalinated water

Whispering and pinching each other, they waited
as each child was served a level ladle of slop.
There were ten children per row, and every one
was numbered, monitored and marvelled at
by the attending medical professionals; in the back,
separated by a thin partition, the kitchen help
swayed to the muffled radio, Louis Armstrong's
"A Kiss to Build a Dream On."

At an elementary school three blocks west,
everyone was elbow deep in a duck-and-cover
drill of their own: recommended defence rehearsals
against atomic attack from the Soviet Union,
a small price to pay for the promise of free electricity,
unlosable golf balls and the all-inclusive stadium
tours in Nevada where the cost of a pair of sunglasses
bought you an unobstructed view of above-ground
weapons testing, of peaceful nuclear explosions.

SONNET XXII

for Finn

Very early in the morning, around 5 o'clock a.m.,
I heard you shuffle out of the bed you had been
sharing with my mother — your Oma — and begin
the search for me through the dark house. I heard
you whisper my name and your sweat-damp feet
catch your graceless steps on the wood floors.
Then, the way people sometimes describe
a shock of unexpected gratitude, I saw the light
from the mechanical toy solar system tucked
between your ribs and arm; in its beams, a hundred
tiny blue stars scattered along the hallway,
and then slowly, as you rounded the corner,
they stretched into the room where I lay waiting,
now holding my breath for you to spot me.

DISAMBIGUATION

for A.M.

It wasn't exactly on this day, and it isn't exactly true,
but what I remember best is the burnt yellow field
you imagined taking me to, the shameless, open sky;
the long and ragged mulch path that would eventually,
if we could wend on long enough, if we had the guts,
lead to the bay and the entrance of the bleached harbour
where you housed your future. *There are no boats here*, you say.
*There is no horizon, and no salient angle of land, gathering
to some distant point that might guide our eye, peripherally,
toward the edge of this place.*

Because I could never understand your metaphors,
and because your hand was warm in my hand, I resolved
to look down instead of panning the length of the scene,
however desperate to locate the brink, the hook, the rim
where the skirt of your future, harboured here, might
meet, might coalesce out of this slip and into
the ground beneath us, the bedrock we stood on,
where the water pooling the scoop in the crag at my feet
was not clear or peaceful as you had hoped, but instead
appeared a microcosm of fecund sea life,

rank and potent, thin sheets of soggy malachite slime
breeding and multiplying along the jagged rock, carved
and cleaved by centuries of geological shifts, by the garrulous
and cruel pecking of seabirds as they teem and abrade
their prey like guerrilla infantry, surrounding then wasting
the shimmering minnows trapped in the dips, gathered in shallow
rock pockets where the tide had abandoned them.
I kept my eyes lowered to my feet, my head bowed until
the curb of the sea no longer arrested my thoughts, until it
became nothing more than a tickle at the hem of my mind.

THERE ARE SPARROWS AT YOUR WINDOW

I think of you in the permanent unfreedom
of a young Seneca weeping not over parts, but over wholes;
You are every train wreck marking an extraordinary day,
you are every last time, every true turning away:

I want you to touch the knotted, burning seams
in your chest again. I want your weeping to be urgent
and outrageous. In full exasperation, and pinned against
the towering reality that *life goes on*, I want you to do
what anyone would do — open jaw and howl.

In my dream you are standing as a park attendant,
pouring sheets of warm water over an ice rink in the dark.
You are enchanted and soothed by the glistening, quiet crawl
of the flood, of the cracking earth shifting under the weight
of the frozen water, the hardened soil. I see you kneeling
at this place, like that, on every occasion.

OUR WEDDING DAY

for Matt

When you forget, I'll remind you. I'll describe something
about the flowers, or the leaves on the trees. I'll tell you
something about the weather, about what that means.
Do you remember now? When you took my face
in your hands, firm where you stood, as soft
as you could (I think you remember now)
you said, "My name means clearer
of the woods." I whispered back —
only you could hear (for the rain
and the thunderclap were near) — I
said, "My name means the place
between, my name means
the trap."

You remember now. It was a lovely
ceremony. No one we knew
was there.

THE DRAMATIST AND HIS
DIALOGUE WITH THE DEVIL

Imagine we ran ourselves right off the road.
It's a bit easy, but it might be very near the truth:
during those times — especially those times —
that you thought you had been winning all along,
imagine you weren't even close.

Imagine we could be luminously sane
and dragooned by only a few minutes to go,
pull off an apology for everything.
A doctrine of explanations. Propositions at best.
Imagine this as a punishment from me to you.

PART
—2—

PUT ANOTHER WAY

For miles and miles, as you can see,
are dark things that follow beside
the place you have come to know me.
These shadowy ships will moor all night
and don't leave — but from time to time,
and though it draws a very thin line,
we might look the other way for a while.

CELEBRATION

Every Tuesday and Thursday morning, across
the street as I wait for the bus in the dark,
I see you on the second floor, naked, illuminated
only by the dim glow of your computer screen.
We are several months in, and I still can't help
but to board the bus and monitor the gazes of others,
braced if one so much as glances your way.

If you asked me what was *wrong*, I couldn't tell you.
But it's not unlike that driftwood-lined image
of thirty-two or thirty-three long-finned pilot whales
beached, horizontal, Indian file along the shore
of the Farewell Spit in Golden Bay.
Their round bodies reflecting every blinding sunbeam,
every baffling act of unmitigated devotion.

SONNET X

for Nate

The lazy morning riled me toward chores
as I collected the socks from underneath
the couch, unfolded and sorted the plastic-wrapped
laundry tower, and unhinged the coffee cup
from the bottom of the wide porcelain plate
from the residue last night's dinner has left.
I unlocked the patio door, a chore sometimes
because the latch is old and temperamental,
revealing a new layer of snow covering
the entranceway. The pale padding skimmed
the layers underneath and reminded me of you.
Of all the mistakes I could have made, but did not.

GOD'S WHIP

There's a scientific lampoon posturing the unknown unknown —
that is, the things we do not know we don't know, angling
our known knowns and our known unknowns. Pauli's was a
    mystery neutrino,
the smallest of small material, without mass and *superluminal*.
    He sensed
its presence in every laboured, secretive tryst in the lab.
    He could know
its properties, its magic. All he had to do was prove it.

He is known to have said of the neutrino, and with a wide
smile, "Its beauty is so immense, or rather, my feeling for it
    so beautiful,
as to cause in me the most persistent, most intense unrest,
the magnitude of which allows me no peace." Later he wrote,
    "I am tired
of looking. I have lost the confidence that it will, that it can,
    be found,"
born, I can only imagine, from thorough exhaustion.

On anxious nights I whisper, *Pauli, sometimes I drink myself to sleep*
like you. I have also tugged at loose hair, administering a small pain
amidst the waves of pleasure, to prove to myself that all beauty
is ugly too, that all desire is fear and that all answers are the friction
birth of all new questions. When I sense I have gained his trust
I move quickly to the point, and gently:

Pauli, how did it feel to learn that your known unknown
was finally a known known? His answer is different every time.
But last night, after your rough exit from me and from our bed,
when your footsteps were gone at the end of the hall,
I heard him. *The truth is, how it felt is a long story,*
and it's late, and you're tired. You've been tired for far too long.

VARIANT C

There once was a blind kid who comforted himself
daily with a dial tone, cradled a plastic phone
to his ear for hours, who later became the freak
midday-calling the Russian foreign embassy
pretending to be a radio talk-show host, inviting
the Soviet on air for a round of American trivia,

tugging conversation and teasing out talks
for as long as possible to give tracers the time
to find him, arrest him and provide him a bed.
This was the 1950s, before the effects of sound
on the human psyche were investigated with
the panache they are now. Before a car horn

in F sharp was standardly applied to all new vehicles,
and the minor second interval was enthusiastically
assigned to rear-moving, heavy-load Mack trucks.
At that time, a dial tone was just a telephony signal
indicating that the exchange was working,
confirming the off-hook, ready to transmit a call.

SAVAGE

HUMBERT: *What are you eating?*
LO: *It's called a jawbreaker. It's supposed to break your jaw. Want one?*

In an unusual instance of stillness and economy,
and after filling a water glass in a sleepwalk,
Lo hovered near the centre of the bedroom window,
coming to. In this light you could make out her soft
arm hair, fine bleached peach fuzz, even her clean
blue eyes and the space the light took up in them.

Her thin nightgown, transparent now, hung from
a distracted hand fisting the cotton and exposing
the secret shapes beneath. She turned to face him,
clumsy and insincere, replacing the glass on the sill.
It is these instances, these gestures alone that declare
so openly the violence of his desire, however perfect.

THE LIGHT I'VE SEEN IN YOUR HAIR
I HAVE FOUND IN MY OWN HANDS

I still hear rumours about the dead fox
we found nailed backward and upside down
from the rafters of Jenny's tool shed
at least three or more summers ago.
The rusted nailheads, its entry wounds,
were tucked from view beneath the slim
lip where the roof meets the open air.
It did not occur to me then we were stealing.
The jury-rig of the undiminished memory,
tripped up by emergency, is the steady
nursing of the conditional — the tedious
combinations of all possible outcomes.
That summer I told you *no* instead of *almost*.
I should have said *very very close*.

IN THE BACKSEAT OF YOUR CAR,
ALL THINGS BEING WHAT THEY ARE

I have measured myself against the winters
of my first home, the perseverance through
which I have fought the kind of gratitude
only snow-trapped isolation can bring.

I have measured myself against the seascapes
and mountain beds of my second home,
against the distant drift and muscling breakwater
that pushes past the edges of all possibility.

I can picture the world being blown apart too,
and then cobbled back together again.
I am picturing those fractured scraps of light
reflect and spin a trillion tiny sun-bullets.

SONNET XVI

Open your eyes and face me. Draw
your free hands from your pockets
and turn your pirate jaw down more.
Sink every penny on the long shot
and quit staring, it's psychopathic.
Unfasten these high horses and give
up the paper route. Of that I'm sure.
Rake up those newsprint, science-fair
remodels and build them higher.
Think about the kids and stop bitching
so loudly, so longly, into half-hung
closet doors between adjoining rooms.
Talk better. Say more things and be
easier on people. I'm not mad.

THE ADULTERER

On particularly busy days, I leave the washing up
until the end of the day, into the evening, because
by then the air is cool and the soap-water in the sink
remains warm to the touch. The house is quiet save for
the low, hand-held radio heard from the neighbour's yard,
and with the window open and the sink positioned
where it is, a breeze will wind in and wrap itself around
my feet and up my legs, along my back. I line the drying
rack with the rinsed plates first, then cups, then any pots
or big pans on top. Alongside everything goes the cutlery.
Not always, but often I have used the broken blue mug
in the morning and have left it all day in the sink to be
washed last of all. The truth is it can't really be used —
whatever goes in just falls back out through the crack.

FOR THE SORA RAIL

Call-broadcasts are catcalls among the cattails: the bait
meant to glimpse, if only for a second or two, its soft
underbelly or yellow ankle or oranging beard.

This one is caught outside a dry wheat field,
out on his own and a fair stretch from the soppy marshland
he must have travelled from.

Look at this because it reminds me of you, or at least
of your pain, which I take as my own.
As I have done, watch without looking away even once.

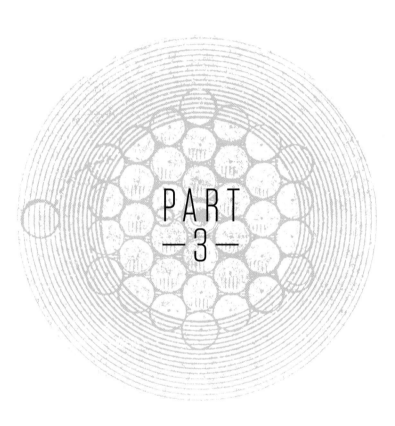

PART
—3—

LISTEN, JUNEBUG

The day you were born, the recession was a real thing,
was really happening, even though Moscow and Istanbul
were seeing significant real estate booms. A pair of bombings
killed fifteen in Pakistan, and Spain tilted a little to the middle.
Attorney General Spitzer, a polarizing and crusading man,
was running a prostitution ring in the Midwest, while Israel began
its ceasefire talks and Fat Joe the rapper had admitted to tax fraud.

This was the day Barack Obama abandoned Hillary Clinton
and ran for leader of the Democratic Party — soon to be the first
black president in US history. Then late in the day, the scientific
community announced that non-human primates conveyed
meaning through call combinations, or morphemes, which are
linguistically defined as the smallest meaningful units in language;
for example, a prefix such as *pre-* or a word such as *I*.

RENFREW, ONTARIO, 1988

From the false and woozy files of my early life
is the figure of a sick and suicidal cow,
mercy-shot near the furthest line of property
owned by my aunt and uncle. I don't know
these people well, but the uncle gave me wads

of yarn to muck with, encouraging a creative
freedom I was unaccustomed to at the time
and exploited without hesitation or constraint.
He must've taken the rifle from the side shed
before his wife woke up. He must've distressed

the plan for some time and he must've assumed
I had not yet awoken from my sleepwalk switch
— from the barn to the inside couch — or he might
have put the lousy chore off at least another day.
The cow broke two legs in a fall six days before

so had stopped eating as a course of prudence
or to speed up the inevitable. It was still dark,
but the sunrise light was coming up quick,
anyone could see. The blow between the eyes
was loud and she hit the ground without a fuss.

I was the same age or this was the same year
the white dog took to amusing itself on the thin
spring ice of the Madawaska River, miles north
of the main house, sliding and trapezing huge
distances, until the afternoon he fell through,

failing to be rescued by the yellow dog or by
any of us. There are saturated colour photos
of this spring, the river and of us by the barn.
I recall the afternoon the white dog drowned
and the morning the lame cow was murdered,

but I can't be sure if my uneasiness with dogs
developed before or after that time, nor whether
I slept on this or that side of the wide screen door
the evenings after — a loosened childhood privilege
that tended to separate seasons at the farm.

THIS IS WHAT IT'S LIKE NOW

Him, in the morning, same
as last night, still soaked
in yesterday's commemoration
of what we both know is coming,

coffee run, Apple Cinnamon
Cheerios and soy milk,
dress, wash, our hands, face.
Walk to the junior public school,

negotiate our way through new
alliances (ours), new enemies (hers),
all the while keeping cool heads,
heeling up against panic,

the drop-off, the kiss-off, the wave.
Let's take a breath and talk like adults.
Let's hold hands and grin.
Let's make long silences

because what we do now, say or don't say,
lays to waste what came before,
builds and rebuilds all that we were,
what we have been all along.

NO ONE IS LOOKING

for Evie

Let's get lit in a dirty pub
with the kind of lighting that makes us
younger and more beautiful than we are.
We'll be urged to split after a table
of brittle scenesters scout us out
with sideways eyes. Stir some contact.
We'll be moved by their demands
on our attention and we'll stay instead
for a round of gamy indiscretion,
which is not the same as love.

Let's get used to everything,
like old folks in pink houses who wake
up at dawn, talk half as often and hardly
ever electrify a room. We'll be amused
by apolitical digressions, tacky jokes
and suicidal pop songs by bipolar girls.
One day, we'll get over *injustice*, learn
to compromise, water the fucking plants
and sleep through the night, which I doubt
is exactly the same as sane.

GIRLCHILD

On our walks home from school,
I keep one eye open for a pine cone,
knowing that if I spot one before you do
and present it for your tiny hands to marvel at —
its size, its rough edges, its special shape —
that in no time, you'll hurl it from the buggy,
forgetting it before it hits the ground.
From your bright eyes and bell-giggle, this taunt:

dole out equally love and loss;
toss-on, you mock, *toss-off.*

FOR OLIVER

This was going to take a Jacob's ladder
— not the Jacob accompanied by his angels,
but the travelling arc — a continuous train
of upward sparks. We'd already assembled
a bucket of grain dust for the homemade
Catherine wheels we'd detonate by the lake.
A spotlit corridor not to heaven, but higher.

On our way to the lake we gathered up,
separately, everything we knew about love
and pushed it out from our buzzing middles.
The youngest and most sincere of us gripping
hard the small boxcar in her pocket, enough
to bruise the bright skin beneath her clothes.
Her advance so protective, persistent, hostile.

HAPPY BELATED WORLD ACCORDION DAY

An accordion party, Gorky Park, Russia,
and by the looks of it, the women have
outnumbered the men by far. The men
are making up the difference in enthusiasm,
though, especially the man in the centre,
holding a five-foot-long accordion
stretched open completely and loosely slung
between his outstretched arms.
Who knows if he's playing it or holding it,
all I can see is his splayed body,
his closed eyes and the separate song he hears
replaying, replaying, replaying somehow.

IT WAS NICE TO SEE YOU AGAIN

Knowing that nothing is free, I recognized early
my shifting physiology, the changes in atmosphere.
Familiarity slid in, so much thinner and higher
in the veins than blood, and I knew again
the toll for things that have been, for those to come.

But I know now how to carry the weight of you,
how to level it evenly across both shoulders,
let it castigate all tenderness, let it sink and settle.
I know now how to bear your beauty too; ·
bitterly and unfreely, but I do.

SONNET XV

If you could sit from me at arm's-length,
at touching-length, and talk as though
not every word you uttered sent tiny
cracks around the globe, splitting the thin
glove the world is packed into —
If you could say what spins inside your
laboured mind, and heart, and bones,
as though not every second passing in talk
erects the burden of injustices, to me, to you,
grainier and duller every time,
would you take my hand in yours, lacing
our fingers, press your skin against mine,
and holding us there unhurried, would you
know that your words on fire are just a fire?

SEQUENCING

If the temperature is temperate, breezy
and warm by the right measurement,
and the leaves are teasing themselves
to life, pulling and rocking their branches
at a particular tug-angle, left left right,

if I'm separated enough that the sound
of nearby chatter or birdsong or dog-bark
can only be heard by fully concentrating,
having been drowned to death by a sudden
and urgent focus on my heartbeat, or scrape

of twig sharp against my exposed ankle,
then I have accumulated by accident
the precise conditions necessary to recall —
and with blooming clarity — my own love,
for just long enough to forgive you.

IT'S LATER THAN YOU THINK

for Andy

Resolve that this is home: the bud bursting
from the maple across the street is the shepherd
you've prayed beside for weeks, however chagrin,
however discreet, and not just because of this
or just because of me, but to re-render and then
later to believe, all that comes between.

This is the fiendishly jerry-built kludge
to end all endless disputes. Take from this
a nuisance of beauty meant for you alone:
here is a boast of small and rusty passerine birds,
claw-foot, landing at the base of the maple tree
to kick up rainwater between their toes.

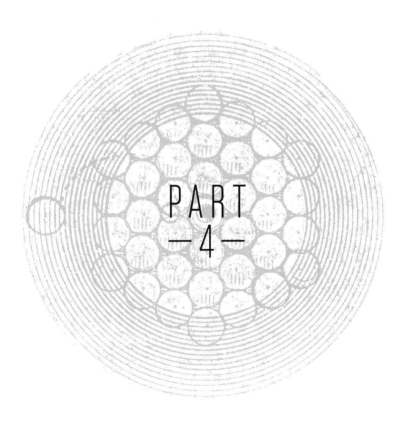

PART
—4—

HONGERWINTER

Infantry Depot, Amersfoort, Nederlanden, 1 September 1949
Re: Krop. Van Veen, Paulus, Born: Zutphen, between wars, 20 June 1926
Residence: Amsterdam, Hair: Blond, Eyes: Blue, Sex: Male, Status: Dutch
Occupation: Plasterer, Dependents: 0, Siblings: 5, Living Parents: 2

At the outset of *Hongerwinter*, the three
hiked to their birthplace of Zutphen,
a hundred and twenty kilometres east,
to lodge with maternal grandparents
until food supplies returned to the capital.

They packed knapsacks with woollen
blankets, thin yellowing bars of SmallBoy,
clothing and tightly sealed water. They took
care to avoid all highways, swarming now
with the occupation and Allied aerial strafing.

They culled the hospitality of farm owners,
and by nightfall on the first day, and with
forty kilometres behind them, they chose
a barn outside of Amersfoort to unfold
and spread their blankets on the straw.

A FACT AS I KNOW IT

The running ahead, and fast,
was the easiest thing they did,
then the gun — he wouldn't hold a gun,
drove ambulances instead —
reminded him of when he met his
wife, Amersfoort, 1944, a stake
of two packs of smokes and a dance.
It was like-like at first sight.

Three bullets missed him, and two
landed flush between the left-side ribs
of his partner, knocking the wind out
for good. Then click clack smackety smack,
like the reel to reel of an eight-track,
like *Casablanca* without a vertical hold,
the quietest fingers creased
the world's most impossible fold.

FORWARD

Did I ever tell you the one about T B?
None of this is unfair nor is it surprising,
but there he is, sheltered from the hard
ruby sun inside the dingy white Red Cross
tent. The first of the many trailing wounded
is a thirty-something woman with T B —
and a nasty set of lesser ailments by
comparison — being handled up the laneway
toward the tent. She's coughing and it's
hot, and phlegm is collecting and spilling
from her every opening: *Do you have T B yet?*
He shakes his head no, and with that she
gathers up and spits out her next mess
of human mire, aiming as close to his mouth
and eyes as possible, the nearest and most
efficient passageways to infection.

SHAKEDOWN

Picture two, maybe three,
halcyon horses. They stand
partly facing the back fence
and partly facing each other.

They lean toward the back
to edge up against the chance
they'll need to split. The risk
one gets spooked enough.

They keep each other in sight
to participate, or to seem so,
and to toy with the idea
of communal solidarity.

But I know, and so do you,
that the second there's alarm,
a quick sound over or underfoot,
they're lunging at all angles.

JUBILEE

As if God were on our side, we give away,
and freely, the things we once loved, perhaps
monstrous in scope now, fermata in *this* form.
The hullabaloo and foofaraw of the hoi polloi

still comes as a clean light, however shop-soiled,
is as beautifully pointless as a merciless mercy kill —
here *mercy* means to weigh in from the outside,
bathos being the full range of the opposite.

It is now we might sleep and fit, growl and wait,
here, and largely because the angle of your
arm while resting distracts me from eating,
and because the bridge of your nose is perfect

in this light, in every light, I can well recognize
the spin the world has in you. Kismet well.

WILLIGHAGEN'S "O MIO"

It's snowing in such an obvious way,
reminding me of the Chinese laundry
in brown paper sacks, the twist-tied,
unsigned, thankfully undated inventory,
always a *sfumato* at pickup. Our lazy

woolgathering is often a zero-emission
experiment, knapped in only minor
degrees by the template of cooked-up,
but polite, customer service. In the fore,
the ancient bedding and plaster jackets

of competent alchemists, pyrotechnists,
hobbyists and adventurers, hang clinging
to full body capes of protective plastic
as birch bark–tar to stone and plant ash,
as 16,500 nerve fibres jaw to synapses,

tinderboxes ratcheting improvements,
marvels, orgies of iconoclasms agitating
against, leveraging a crush-rub anent
the small tip-change in my badly broken
and soiled (the irony) fleece pockets.

BREAD AT AUGUSTFEHN

in memoriam Paul Van Veen

By the spring, Nazi victory was hopeless;
tabs being kept on the captured were slight,

soon to be abandoned altogether. If one
managed escape, little was done to retrieve

him, so I can imagine the German girl tossing
a half loaf of bread over a nearby perimeter

fence, diminishing as a means of confinement,
for my grandfather to pilfer and hide for later.

It's easier still to imagine him stashing it under
bricks and rubble, as he did, and relieved his

brother was recovering from illness, and to cheer
him even further, relaying the details of the day's

unexpected gift, stored from sight and marked
by twigs in the shape of an uneven *V*.

The next day he snuck back to the spot to tear
a fistful from the undetected loaf, rationing

the remainder as insurance for at least a while
longer. He may have known then, and certainly

in the moments that followed — having been
spotted and overpowered by fellow inmates —

the nature of desperation from both sides now,
and with growing concern, the ongoing hazards

of his own compassion, only to be tested again
months later, and after a successful escape from

the camp, when his travelling partner, aware of
the sliced bread and dried strips of bacon tucked

inside his carryall, deserted him while he slept,
having cabbaged his sack and canteen of water.

Imagine too, after many days, he reached the
relief tent near the border, exhausted and weak,

convinced he was hallucinating when he was led
by two luminous nurses in stiff uniforms to a small

room containing only a square piece of thick paper
taped to the floor and a wicker basket. Caretakers

spoke kindly, instructing him to deposit what he
owned into the bin so as to easily strip him of his

clothes, rife with muck and lice, and bathe him
thoroughly with soap and DDT. Soon after drying,

he was given new clothing to continue the walk
from Assen to Hasselt to Zutphen, crying in now

uncontainable joy, and soon to be reunited with
his family, as skinny or skinnier than he.

These are some of the stories he told me when
I was young, and in more detail as I grew older.

He asked me once to take his notes, written in bad
English, and to put those years together in some

order so everyone would know, but that was before
he died and when I didn't know why he'd asked *me*.

THE PSYCHIC

All My Friends Are Funeral Singers is led by a non-actress
who plays a tarot card–reading medium living in an old white
house, irritatingly occupied by a jumble of old white ghosts

which more or less keep to themselves in the top east-side
bedroom, also white, playing drums and guitars 'til all hours.
As you can guess, this habit causes a certain level of unease

for the only living tenant, and over the course of the film,
she is forced to reimagine her daily goings-on, as she is left
with little other option but to work with the poltergeists

in an unwilling but firmly necessary union. Sleeping remained
a continual problem, however, as the band insisted on late-night
jams, but by the end all is hopeful, except for a few unsurprising

hiccups, and the ghosts dance with the psychic: a jarring choir
of misfits around the hallucination of a backyard firepit. None
of this is real, it's a movie, but I did meet the non-actress, non-

psychic when her ghost band — and a convoy of paying onlookers —
came to my house to play songs in my living room years later;
she sold me a T-shirt and gifted me a poster, but didn't warm to me

until late in the night, and only after I'd shared photos of my child
dancing, spinning and laughing in her wrinkled white nightgown,
her hair still a matted mess from a fitful sleep the night before.

SUN DOG COMMUNITY GARDEN

This is the shabby garden of brimful sensibility,
of copious anonymity and of ravenous reactivity.
I am surveyor of bird and briar, of bloom taxonomy,
descendant of thorough and uncertain emblemology.

Here, jungle brush is as good a starting place as any
to all erogenies, to earthly terms, to bawdy philosophies.
I am encounterer and recorder of civic natural order,
employer and mourner of every private corner.

ACKNOWLEDGEMENTS

Thanks to Nathaniel G. Moore, Jeff Latosik, Lindsay Coleman, Spencer Gordon, Jowita Bydlowska, Hillary Rexe, Jon Hastings, Mathew Henderson, Alexis Von Konigslow, Matt Rader and Paul Vermeersch for your early reading and encouragement.

I'd also like to acknowledge the generosity and support of the Ontario Arts Council in the making of this book.

NOTES

"It's Later Than You Think" previously appeared in *CV2*. "For the Sora Rail," an earlier version of "Listen, Junebug" and "Renfrew, Ontario, 1988" appeared in *The Humber Literary Review*. "The Adulterer" appeared in *subTerrain*. "Victory Lap," "This Is What It's Like Now" and "A Fact As I Know It" appeared in *Forget Magazine*. "Variant C" and an earlier version of "A Wager" appeared in *The Rusty Toque*. "Table Talk" and "Disambiguation" appeared in *Emerge Literary Journal*. "Peace" and "Our Wedding Day" appeared online in *fwriction : review*, and "Celebration" and "God's Whip" appeared in *The Puritan*.

Amber McMillan teaches English literature and writing. *We Can't Ever Do This Again* is her first collection of poetry. McMillan lives on Protection Island, BC, with her partner, daughter and two cats.